Steve Parish

WESTERN AUSTRALIA

Contents

▶▶

page 1: Red and Green Kangaroo Paw *Anigozanthos manglesii* is the State floral emblem.
pages 2 and 3: Cape Leeuwin, where ships "turn the corner" between the Indian and Southern
Oceans. *opposite:* The Salmon Holes in Torndirrup National Park on the coast south
of Albany, named for the big schools of salmon that come into the bay.

Introduction

▶▶

Western Australia is a vast place. Australia's largest State occupies one-third of the continent. From the jagged coastline and monsoon plains of the Kimberley, the towering Karri forests and rugged granite headlands of the southern coast, the unique limestone pillars of The Pinnacles on the Coral Coast, to the marvellous marine life of Ningaloo Marine Park and Shark Bay, this is a place filled with natural wonder and beauty.

Much of Western Australia's interior is unforgiving desert, and the soils of the well-watered south-west corner are not rich in plant nutrients. Yet, every springtime, especially after good winter rains, the red aridlands are carpeted with wildflowers and the coastal plains and sandy heathlands are ablaze with blossoms of all colours, shapes and textures. Many of Western Australia's approximately 8000 species of wildflowers are found nowhere else in the world.

Visitors to Western Australia may discover unspoilt beaches and rugged ranges that, until recent years, were unknown to all but a few, and remain much as they have for thousands of years, without human intervention. Yet, is also possible to journey from place to place, savouring the best of accommodation, wonderful food and the warmest of hospitality. Perth, the capital city, and its companion port, Fremantle, on the broad banks of the Swan River, are modern centres of commerce and industry in which magnificent restaurants and sophisticated entertainment can be found. Even the smallest country towns have their own welcoming lifestyles.

This is a State that owes its prosperity to vast mineral deposits, agriculture and the pastoral industry. It is also rich in culture and human resources. Its people have forged a self-reliant society that enjoys its natural heritage and is always happy to share its good fortune with interstate and international visitors.

opposite: York, a farming town 90 kilometres east of Perth, was established in 1831. The carefully preserved historic buildings such as these along Avon Terrace, are a source of great pride to the town.

Around Perth

This chapter covers only a very small part of the huge state of Western Australia. But this small area holds not only most of Western Australia's population, but also many of its buildings of interest and historic sites, its main sporting facilities, and most popular beaches and resort islands.

For Perth and Fremantle, the Swan River has always been the focus from coast to hills. The river was the site of earliest west coast settlement, and today provides not only a magnificent scenic background to city and suburbs, but also a site for yachting and other water activities on its wide estuary-like lower reaches. Despite the river's proximity to the city, it is still possible to go fishing and crabbing within sight of the tall city buildings. At parts of the river where there are exposed sandbars, large numbers of waterbirds and migrant waders gather. Elsewhere, parklands come down right to the water's edge.

Overlooking the river and Perth's city centre is Kings Park. Established in 1872, the park features a large area of natural bushland and a magnificent botanic garden with diverse displays of the best of Western Australia's famous wildflowers, and has long been a favourite picnic spot for both locals and visitors.

The port city of Fremantle is known for its great number of well-preserved historic buildings and the opportunity for waterfront seafood dining. In sight of Fremantle, to the west on the Indian Ocean horizon, are Rottnest and Garden Islands, which, with their associated reefs, shelter much of this part of the coast, giving a large area of protected waters. Rottnest Island is the West's most popular offshore holiday centre, with lovely scenery, beaches, fishing, cottages and other accommodation, and no traffic.

opposite: Looking over Matilda Bay, the Swan River and the Narrows to Perth city.
pages 10 and 11: Magnificent views of the city and the Swan River are framed by native flower gardens in Kings Park on the slopes of Mt Eliza.

opposite: An aerial view of Perth city. Kings Park can be seen at bottom left.
above: Undoubtedly the best view of the city is from Kings Park.

opposite: The Flame of Remembrance and the War Memorial, which are situated on the edge of the steep escarpment in Kings Park, command a clear view over the city and river.
above: The native floral clock is planted annually as a herald to spring.

above: The Lotterywest Federation Walkway allows visitors to walk amidst the tree canopies.
opposite: The Pioneer Women's Memorial Fountain is in the heart of Kings Park.

pages 18 and 19: Visitors to Kings Park Botanic Gardens can see a diversity of wildflowers from all over Western Australia. It would take many months and thousands of kilometres of travel to most parts of this huge State to see these flowers in their natural habitats.

above: The simple lines of Hay Street Mall's modern street lights contrast with the ornate detail of Perth Town Hall's clock tower.

above: Built in 1937, the mock-Tudor facade of London Court surrounds a narrow pedestrian thoroughfare between the Hay Street Mall and St Georges Terrace.

above: It is more than 30 years since traffic flowed though this section of Hay Street. Nowadays, the pace is more relaxed.

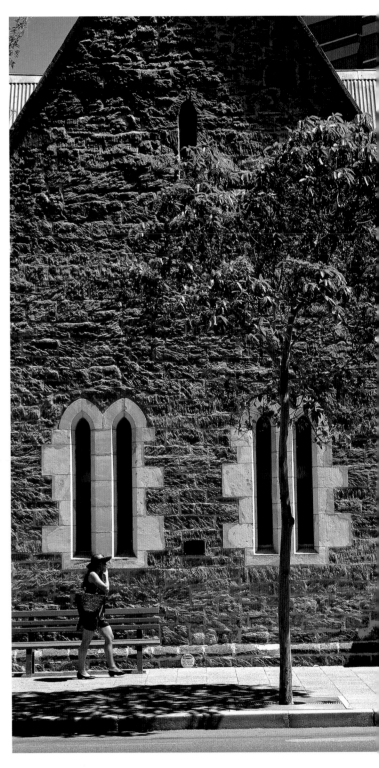

above: Established in 1899 to make gold sovereigns for the British Empire, the Perth Mint is Australia's oldest operating mint. National Trust-listed, the mint now produces commemorative medallions and coins in precious metals.

above: The University of Western Australia's Winthrop Hall was built in 1932. This imposing building features a tall, rectangular clock tower, and the main hall is supported on the slender columns and arches of an open undercroft.

above: Built in 1854, the stone for the Old Perth Boys School was ferried up-river by convict labour. One of the oldest buildings in Perth, the restored site is listed by the National Trust. Today, it is used by the Trust as an information centre and shop.

![Trinity Church]

above: Some of Perth's most significant heritage sites are now protected within the Malls Heritage Precinct. One such site is magnificent Trinity Church, which has graced St Georges Terrace since 1894.

above: Completed in 1870, Wesley Uniting Church was built at the same time as Perth's City Hall, with the same construction team working both jobs. Behind the church towers the metal and glass structure of Central Park.

above: Forrest House was the home of Alexander Forrest, the explorer and former Lord mayor of Perth. This reconstruction was built near the original house's location, now surrounded by modern office towers.

above: Subiaco Oval is conspicuous for its four floodlight towers. The stadium has long been the home of Australian Rules football in Western Australia, but now hosts international Rugby matches as well.

above: Australian cricketer Brett Lee bowls. In Western Australia the "WACA" (the West Australian Cricket Association ground) is the venue for interstate and international cricke[t]

above: An aerial view of the "WACA". These grounds were officially opened in 1893 and in 1970 Western Australia's first Ashes Test match was played here.

top and above: Between the city and river is a long, wide green belt of lawns, sports fields and gardens, providing colour and natural beauty to the city's centre, as well as peaceful spots to escape the city's hustle and bustle. One such sanctuary is the Heritage-listed Esplanade.

above: Kangaroo sculptures are a recent addition to Stirling Gardens. The gardens were originally used for the acclimatisation of plants brought to the new colony from Europe, and was where many now-old trees were grown from seed, as were grape and fruit trees. The garden's stone walls and pools were added in 1965.

above: At Burswood, an arresting sculpture of five Black Swans, representing the five categories of the Citizen of the Year award, is set in a fountain. In 2001 a cygnet was added to the group, representing youth recipients of the award.

above: Real Black Swans float on a pool below Kings Park, close to the central city towers. Although now found mainly on small ponds and lakes, in 1697 the birds were present in such numbers on the open waters of the Swan River, that the Dutch navigator Willem de Vlamingh named the river for them.

this page: At the Perth Zoo, imaginative signposting indicates the location of various exhibits. A Sumatran Tiger ambles through vegetation much like that found in its homeland. The zoo, opened in 1898, has evolved into a place where visitors can see animals from around the world and learn about their natural habitats.

opposite: Together with the Black Swan, at top, the Numbat is one of Western Australia's two faunal emblems. A small termite-eating marsupial, the distinctively-striped Numbat is now so rare that its range is limited to a few small areas in south-western Western Australia.

this page: Swan Bells was built as Perth's Millennium Project, and houses a set of bells given to the city. Towards the base, the inner spire is partly enclosed by a leaf-like sheath, which appears to open to allow the spire to soar towards the sky.

above: From the air, the bell tower stands out above the green gardens of the Esplanade. The graceful tower's slender, rounded shape contrasts with the angular lines of the city buildings beyond.

above: A sculpture of a Perth icon, the Black Swan, stands on the Barrack Square walkway with another icon, the Swan Bells, in the background. The tower's peal of 18 bells were a gift from the City of London for Australia's Bicentennial.

above: At a height of more than 80 metres, the spire of the Swan Bells towers over traffic on Barrack Street. When the bells are rung, their beautiful chimes are heard through much of the city.

pages 32 and 33: Small pleasure boats at Matilda Bay, Crawley. *above:* On the western coast north of Perth and Fremantle is Hillarys Boat Harbour. Long lines of boats are moored at Hillarys Marina behind breakwaters that provide protection from the waves and storms that pummel this unsheltered section of coastline.

top: Loggerhead Turtle at AQWA, the Aquarium of Western Australia, which is located at Hillarys Boat Harbour. *above:* Tucked in behind the marina is a sheltered stretch of beach that is the perfect spot to launch a canoe.

above: Cottesloe beach is just north of the entrance to the Port of Fremantle. There is an impressive view of the beach and ocean from the dining room of the elegant Indiana Tearooms, seen at lower left.

above: From the air, the long wide beach of Scarborough can be seen stretching north and south. Beyond the sands are Perth's western suburbs.

top: A small bay complete with a beach of stark white sand, one of many such tucked into Rottnest Island's rocky coastline, is an inviting spot to swim, snorkel and enjoy the sunshine.
above : The larger of the island's two lighthouses is on Wadjemup Hill.

above: On the northern side of the island is Geordie Bay, and, in the foreground, Longreach Bay, with a long curve of white beach and safe mooring sites for small boats.
opposite: Bathurst Point Lighthouse is near to the busy shipping lanes into Fremantle Harbour.

above and opposite: An aerial view north across Fremantle and her four harbours: from below right, is Success Harbour, home of the Fremantle Sailing Club. At bottom left, Fishing Boat Harbour's long jetties are crowded with small craft. Beyond, is Challenger Harbour, built for the America's Cup challenge series in 1987. At top, is Inner Harbour, the Port of Fremantle's commercial shipping dock area.

this page and opposite: A fascinating mix of architectural styles, materials, colours and detailing are found in Fremantle's historic buildings. Many of these fine buildings are classified and protected by the National Trust as magnificent reminders of the port's early prosperity.

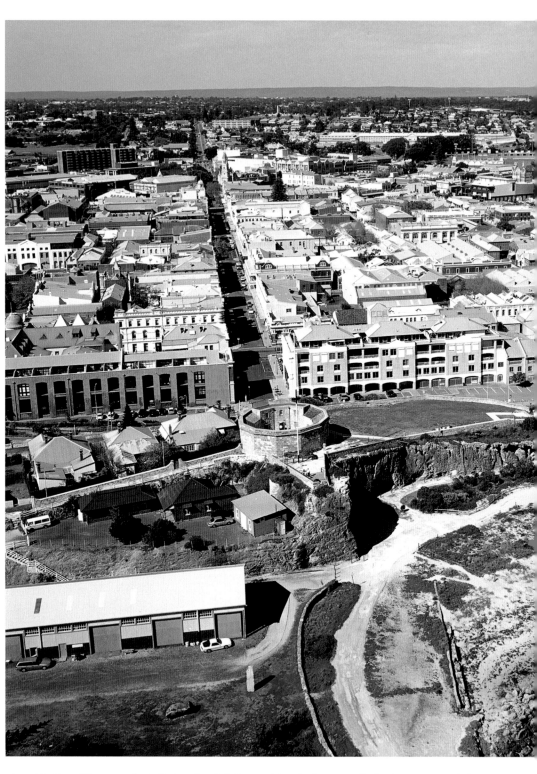

top: The elegant Orient Hotel, in High Street in Fremantle's West End precinct, was established in 1901.
above: A relaxed ambience pervades the Fremantle streets, with many restaurants offering pavement dining.

above: The Round House overlooks Bathers Bay. Built in 1831, it has the honours of being Western Australia's first prison and oldest surviving building. Contrary to its name, the building is octagonal rather than round.

top: The Fremantle Railway Station, completed in 1907, replaced an earlier station built in 1881 in Mouat Street. *above:* The elaborate facades of Fremantle's historic buildings add to the city's charm.

above: Mandurah lies at the meeting point between the Mandurah Estuary
and the Indian Ocean. Peel Inlet is visible in the distance.

above: Boats dot the blue waters of Mangles Bay, off the coast at Rockingham, a resort town just south of Perth.

The South-West

▶▶

While most of Western Australia is dry and hot, the State's south-west corner is unique. Set between the Indian and Southern Oceans, this region has cool, cloudy and often rainy days, even in midsummer. Such a climate has resulted in the region's magnificent flora. Some of Australia's tallest trees grow in the Karri forests here, contrasting with the low, windswept coastal heathlands and a diverse array of wildflowers, many found nowhere else in the world.

The region is bounded on the western and southern sides by spectacular coastline. On the western side, the Indian Ocean crashes against coastal cliffs or rolls softly into shallow, protected estuaries and bays, and spectacular caves. Near the port towns of Bunbury and Busselton, the coastline is low and sandy but becomes rugged between the two Capes – Leeuwin and Naturaliste. It is here, in the south-western corner, that the famed surf beaches of Yallingup and Margaret River are found. Margaret River is also renowned for its vineyards and fine wines.

Along the southern coast, ranges plunge abruptly to the ocean in bold headlands ending at seas as steep, surf-ringed islands. Set between these rocky slopes are white beaches, long lines of dazzling white breakers, and turquoise and azure seas. This scenic coastline is easily seen from the region's coastal national parks. Further east, a succession of ranges create massive headlands, separated by wide bays with kilometres of wide, white beaches. Each has its own distinctive scenery and wildflowers, but share a bird population that includes colourful and rare species.

In the central part of this region are two long lines of jagged peaks. Closest to the former whaling port of Albany is the Porongorup Range, with peaks of granite and pockets of Karri forest. Further north, the saw-tooth silhouette of the Stirling Range dominates the horizon. This series of high peaks is home to many unique wildflowers, some confined to the highest reaches where cloud creates a cool, moist environment quite unlike the surrounding plains.

opposite: Along the south coast, extensive sand plains are clad in heath, with many and varied wildflowers. Here, the huge yellow flower spikes and long serrated leaves of the Bull Banksia, *Banksia grandis*, stand out above the low vegetation.

above: The Heritage-listed Busselton jetty was built in 1865 and closed as a commercial jetty in 1972. It extends almost two kilometres across the shallow bay to deeper water, making it the longest wooden jetty in the Southern Hemisphere. Visitors may walk or take the train to the underwater observatory at the jetty's end to see the corals, colourful fish and other marine life eight metres below the surface.

above: Bunbury's Rose Hotel was built in 1865, but completely rebuilt in 1898 to cater better for the rush of prospectors coming ashore and heading for the goldfields and fortune.

opposite: The Merchant Tea & Coffee Company occupies an elegant old hotel in Busselton.

above: **Near Cape Naturaliste, Sugarloaf Rock is separated from the mainland by a narrow channel through which the swells of the open ocean surge in white foam, even on the calmest days. The rock provides secure roosting and nesting for many seabirds and is a popular spot for birdwatchers.**

above: The lantern room of the Naturaliste Lighthouse is visible above low coastal scrub on Cape Naturaliste. South from here to Cape Leeuwin, Cape Leeuwin–Naturaliste National Park protects a scenic coast of rocky headlands and small sheltered bays, caves and stands of Karri forest.

pages 56 and 57: As the sun drops below an ocean horizon on this western coast, the last golden light silhouettes fishermen casting into calm waters of a protected bay.
page 57, right: the wineries of the Margaret River area are renowned world wide.

opposite: A Long-billed (Baudin's) Black-Cockatoo pauses atop a yellow banksia flower spike.
above: Cafés, hotels, arts and craft shops and galleries line Hampton Street in Bridgetown, which is situated on the banks of the Blackwood River.

pages 60 and 61: Ships sailing near Cape Leeuwin have been guided by the cape's lighthouse since 1896. *pages 62 and 63:* The trees soar to 90 metres in Boranup Karri Forest, Leeuwin–Naturaliste National Park.

above and opposite: The Tree Top Walk in the Valley of the Giants is a 420-metre walkway through the canopy of Red Tingle Trees. The largest of these giant trees have trunks with a circumference of 16 metres at the base.

above: An Australian Pelican watches intently as it floats on the glassy waters of a sheltered estuary.

above: Paperbarks are reflected in the calm surface of the Denmark River and Wilsons Inlet.

above and opposite: Rock is a strong feature along this rugged southern coast, often in cliffs and headlands. Here, in William Bay National Park, the shore's edge is dominated by a cluster of large, grey, round-backed rocks that are aptly named the Elephant Rocks.

opposite: Albany Town Hall is one of the town's oldest and most impressive public buildings.
top: Once the centre of Albany's livelihood, Albany's whaling station is now a museum.
above: Two Peoples Bay is an important reserve for mammals and migratory birds.

top: Waves crash beneath the great stone arch of Natural Bridge, Torndirrup National Park.
above: A clear view of the enclosed waters of Princes Royal Harbour is attained from the top of York Street, the main thoroughfare in Albany.

above: **An aerial view of Torndirrup National Park: in the foreground is Isthmus Bay, the Salmon Holes at centre and Bald Head at bottom right.**

above: Bald Island, at left, is home to a colony of Quokkas. The island is only a
short distance from Waychinicup National Park, at top right, on the mainland.

above: An unusual granite rock formation is enhanced by native wildflowers in Waychinicup National Park.

above: It is ironic that the coastal hills of Fitzgerald River National Park are known as The Barrens.
The area is, in fact, home to more than 1800 plant species – almost a fifth of all the species
found in Western Australia – some of which are only found in this area.
opposite: A Southern Right Whale and her calf swim in Doubtful Bay, near Gordons Inlet.

opposite: The Stirling Range's line of jagged peaks extends 65 kilometres, east to west, above the surrounding flat plains. The entire range is a national park, and rises so abruptly that the highest peaks are often capped in cloud and, occasionally, snow. *above, left to right:* Custard Orchid, *Thelymitra villosa*; Splendid White Spider Orchid, *Caladenia splendens*; Queen of Sheba Orchid, *Thelymitra variegata*.

The Golden Outback

▶ ▶

Western Australia's Wheatbelt extends from Northam and York southwards and curving eastwards through Wagin and Katanning until within sight of the long line of jagged peaks of the Stirling Range, then sweeps east towards the southern coast. These are the open expanses of a vast, gently undulating plateau that has long been the heart of the West's grain and sheep country. Dotted throughout this area are large granite outcrops known as tors, the most impressive being Wave Rock near Hyden.

The fertile and well-watered land of the Wheatbelt was taken up by the first European settlers who could see the land's promise. Their foresight and hard work is evident today in the region's towns, now established for well over a hundred years, many of which proudly display impressive public buildings of stone, proclaiming the region's early prosperity.

Further inland again, the land's promise was not good soil and rainfall for stock and crops, but gold. In the late 19th Century, towns such as Kalgoorlie and Coolgardie sprang to life after rich mining strikes, bringing dramatic population surges and frenzied gold rushes as hopeful prospectors flocked to the region to find a fast fortune.

The riches of the gold rush extended to Esperance, a port on the southern coast. Today, Esperance is an inviting resort, home to a colony of Australian Sea-lions in Esperance Bay, and with five beautiful national parks within easy reach.

opposite: Huge rolls of golden hay are gathered, tied, sheathed in plastic film, and dropped at regular intervals across a vast golden-brown paddock – a sight typical of modern farming with massive modern machinery. On this same land the pioneers, a century or more ago, cut, tied and placed their crops of hay by hand.

above: Even in a town known for its abundance of historic buildings,
York's elaborate and imposing Town Hall is an impressive sight.

above: New Norcia's Spanish-influenced architecture is a lasting reminder of the Benedictine monks who founded a monastery, mission and schools here in 1847.

above: The deep, shady verandahs of Moran's Wagin Hotel invite travellers in to stop for a while. Similar hotels were built in towns throughout the Wheatbelt and goldfields. Their bars would have offered welcome relief from the day's heavy toil, celebrating success or drowning disappointment.

top and above: The sheep depicted in these delightful murals suggest how valuable these animals – in their flocks of thousands on almost every farm – are to the wheat-and-wool economy of this district, the Wheatbelt, and indeed to Western Australia.

Deep, shady verandahs, distinctive street facades, cast iron or wooden detailing, or maybe a colourful mural: although they share similar architectural styles, the pubs and other old buildings of these small towns display a local touch. *opposite:* Katanning. *top:* Pingelly. *above:* Cuballing.

above: A team of Clydesdales proudly lead the way past the Narrogin Town Hall, delivering goods much as they did in pioneering days. In such a vast area, where settlements were far-flung, horse-drawn transport was the lifeline for early settlers.

this page: This region's links with the land, past and present, are found in art and in nature. The landscape is of gently undulating hills, tree-lined winter creeks in the valleys, single trees scattered across the paddocks giving shelter to sheep and cattle, and paddocks bright with flowering canola. Here and there, are cottages, reminders of those who settled here.

above: Quirky embellishments add individual style to this prospector's caravan; in Broad Arrow, the town's namesake tavern still stands as a reminder of the golden glory days.

above: Kalgoorlie's Heritage Precinct is an impressive collection of fine public buildings from the 19th and early 20th centuries that displays the town's gold mining success. Dominating Hannan Street is the Post Office Building. Completed in 1899, the clocktower was set in motion in 1900.

above: The elaborate facade of the Marvel Bar Hotel is a reminder of the immense prosperity enjoyed during the 19th Century heyday of Coolgardie. The gold rush here was short-lived and hopeful prospectors turned to the rich deep veins of gold near Kalgoorlie.

above and opposite: Scattered throughout this region are low, granite hills, weathered and sculptured by wind and water into smoothly contoured, low, overhanging cliffs. Near Hyden is Wave Rock. At more than 100 metres long, and streaked with algae, it is an impressive sight.

above and opposite: Although tractors, utes and motor bikes of various types have replaced the horses that pulled ploughs and provided transport, sheep dogs still prove their worth on almost every farm. Their obedience, speed and knowledge of how and where to shift the flock still make them the essential working companions of every farmer across the golden outback.

top: The Australian Sea-lion is found along Western Australia's southern and western coasts, especially on the rocky shoreline slopes and beaches of islands near Esperance and Albany. *above:* Bays sheltered by headlands and islands provide attractive beaches, some easily reached by well-marked walkways.

top: The long Esperance Jetty. *above:* Swampy parts of the coast have dense paperbark vegetation, providing sanctuary for birds and other wildlife. *opposite:* About 56 kilometres east of Esperance, the rounded granite hills of Cape Le Grande National Park stand above the flat sand plains, dominating this section of coast.

The Coral Coast

▶▶

The Coral Coast is one of sharp contrast and unspoilt beauty, much of it protected within reserves, marine parks and national parks. Within Nambung National Park, some 245 kilometres north of Perth, the eerie limestone landscape of the Pinnacles stand starkly in the desert against the empty sky. Further up the coast lies bustling Geraldton, the region's largest town, a seaside resort and an important centre for the area's fishing industry.

Kalbarri National Park is home to spectacular landscapes, wildflowers and wildlife, and tinted with the many colours of the region's famous Tumblagooda Sandstone. The Murchison River flows through the park's gorges to the Indian Ocean. The magnificent Zuytdorp Cliffs, an immense wall of red rock that towers along the ocean's edge, plunge vertically into the blue water, where, unprotected by islands or reefs, the full force of huge waves crashes repeatedly against the rock.

North of the dizzying heights of the Zuytdorp Cliffs is the Peron Peninsula, including Francois Peron National Park. The land, covered with dense stunted vegetation and vibrant wildflowers, is still a vibrant red, but descends to a low, level landscape edged with white, sandy beaches that slope gently into the brilliant blue waters of Shark Bay.

Shark Bay Marine Park, the State's first World-Heritage-listed site, is home to Dugongs, Manta Rays and turtles, and a number of rare marine animals. At Monkey Mia, on the eastern side of Peron Peninsula, wild dolphins come to be fed, watched by a seemingly endless stream of admirers.

The largest fringing reef in Australia is found in Ningaloo Marine Park, with some reefs so close to the coastline that it is possible to explore the complexities of the coral environment right from the beach. As well as multitudes of colourful reef fish, these waters are also visited by the enigmatic Whale Sharks and Humpback Whales.

opposite: The eerie landscape of the Pinnacles, found in Nambung National Park, where the coastal sand plains meet the Indian Ocean.

above: On Basile Island in the Houtman Abrolhos, 60 kilometres off the coast from Geraldton, fishermen have built shacks. These are their temporary homes on the coral reefs for use between March and June.

Flowers of the west, *above, left to right:* Orange Banksia *Banksia prionotes*, Wreath Lechenaultia *Lechenaultia macrantha*, and Pingle *Dryandra squarrosa*. *opposite, left to right:* Cowslip Orchid *Caladenia flava*, Mottlecah *Eucalyptus macrocarpa*, and Pink Fairy Orchid *Caladenia latifolia*.

above: In Kalbarri National Park, the Murchison River has cut a long, winding gorge to reach the Indian Ocean. Seen here from Hawks Head Lookout, the exposed layers of the sandstone cliffs create striated patterns with alternating layers of brown, white, yellow ochre and red tones.

above: The colour variations of Tumblagooda Sandstone can be seen in the rock layers of the formation known as Nature's Window. *opposite:* For most of the year, the Murchison River is a tranquil chain of pools whose smooth surface creates mirror reflections of red cliffs against overhead blue skies.

pages 108 and 109: The Zuytdorp Cliffs extend north of the mouth of the Murchison River for more than 100 kilometres. This wall of reddish-golden rock rises to 170 metres above the ocean, but in 1712 a few survivors from the wreck of the Dutch ship *Zuytdorp* somehow managed to reach the cliff-top.

above and opposite: At Monkey Mia, a small group of Bottlenose Dolphins come in regularly to be fed, being seen by, and interacting with, visitors to the site. The dolphins, which are part of a much larger group inhabiting Shark Bay, have been coming in to the feeding site for several generations.

above: The rich red soil of the Peron Peninsula produces magnificent displays of
wildflowers in Shark Bay World Heritage Area.

above: To the south and east of Shark Bay, the land is mostly pastoral, with sparse mulga scrub vegetation. After the winter rains, papery flowers carpet the ground in yellow.

above: From the air the dramatic contrast between the red plains and cliffs of the Peron Peninsula and the brilliant blue waters of Shark Bay is seen to its best advantage.

above: On the ground, the view is just as magnificent where the red sands of Francois Peron National Park meet the white sand and blue waters of Shark Bay Marine Park.

opposite: Ningaloo Reef Marine Park is home to an array of marine life and coral reefs. *top:* Yardie Creek Gorge's red limestone cliffs plunge into deep blue water. *above:* The road snakes along almost flat ridges between the gorges of Shothole Canyon in Cape Range National Park.

above: Whale Sharks visit the Ningaloo coast between March and June and often swim close to the surface. The largest shark and largest of all fish, Whale Sharks may reach a length of 12 metres.

above: An abundance of coral, brightly coloured fish and other marine animals may be discovered in the shallows of Ningaloo Reef.

this page and opposite: The largest fringing reef in Australia is at Ningaloo. At some points, the reef is only 100 metres from the shore. More than 180 coral species make the reef a diver's paradise.

The North-West

▶ ▶

The North-West is immense and varied. It covers almost half of Western Australia, and includes both the Kimberley and the Pilbara regions, with landforms ranging from sandy deserts to rugged ranges and climates from arid to wet tropical.

The southernmost part takes in the massive dome of Mt Augustus, a range somewhat resembling Central Australia's Uluru. However, Mt Augustus is larger, and broken by gullies and crevices containing dense stands of trees and shrubs. From the coastal port of Carnarvon, the Gascoyne River spreads its tributaries far inland and widely across the plains and among the ranges of the semi-arid mid west.

Northwards, the Hamersley Range is a great rugged barrier, starting inland of the coast at North-West Cape and sweeping eastwards through much of the Pilbara region to end in the dunes of the Great Sandy Desert. Much of the Hamersley is a huge and ancient plateau, above which rises higher ranges, that include Mt Meharry, Western Australia's highest peak. The long northern face of the Hamersley Range is an imposing, cliff-rimmed escarpment dissected by gorges, including the breathtaking canyons of Karijini National Park.

Northwards again, the Great Sandy Desert, which covers a huge area of the interior of the north-west, sweeps westwards towards the ocean, its sands forming the long, smooth, sweep of coastline known as Eighty Mile Beach lying south of the historic port and pearling community of Broome and the rich beauty of Gantheaume Point and Cable Beach.

Beyond the Great Sandy Desert lies the Kimberley. This is a region dominated by long walls of ranges, huge rivers and vast cattle stations, some as large as a small European country. Together with an almost impenetrable coastline dotted with gorges, waterfalls, and a great many islands and reefs, this makes the place like no other.

opposite: The north-eastern Kimberley is a challenging landscape of rugged, cliff-rimmed ranges, and fast-flowing rivers. Negotiating a path across the Pentecost River Crossing, below the Cockburn Range, requires careful concentration. The hazards of these rivers are increased by the presence of Saltwater Crocodiles.

above: At the end of the day's mustering, stockmen gather as sunset filters through a haze of dust stirred up by the hooves of horses and cattle.

above: On the coast at Cable Beach, the silhouette of a line of camels against the glow of sunset has become one of the best-known images of Broome.

above: The scanty leaves of a Boab tree provide some shade during a break in horseback work on the plains. Whether used during mustering or when inspecting fences, horses are still an important part of outback life.

this page: Fast action is part of a day's work in the saddle. Most of the Kimberley region is rugged, or has vast plains, requiring cattle to be mustered into yards at outstations near watering places.

pages 128 and 129: The low, rocky headland of Gantheaume Point, just south-west of Broome, overlooks Gantheaume Bay. *above and opposite:* North of Gantheaume Point, Cable Beach makes a broad sweep around the turquoise waters of Gantheaume Bay.

above: Lennard River Gorge is on the western side of the King Leopold Ranges.
opposite: The four cascades that make up Mitchell Falls.

opposite: The red rock is reflected in a broad pool above the falls of Bell Gorge in Bell Creek Reserve. *above:* The cascading waterfall drops into a deep gorge.

opposite and above: Boabs are the most distinctive trees of the Kimberley. Also known as "bottle trees" for their shape, these trees are deciduous, and are usually leafless in the cooler dry season. During the summer wet season, Boabs carry a canopy of rich green foliage.

this page, left to right: The Fitzroy River is one of the largest rivers on the Kimberley; the local floodwaters are channeled through Diamond Gorge.

this page, left to right: The eroded jagged limestone top of the Oscar Range was once at sea level; the broad watercourse of the Drysdale River flows northwards to meet the Timor Sea near Kalumburu.

above and opposite: The Kimberley coastline contains some of Australia's most spectacular scenery. From Derby to its most northern point, this is a coast of rough and rugged ranges that meet the sea in high rocky headlands, and deep fjord-like bays, ending in a maze of hilly offshore islands.

above: Still waters reflect the handiwork of the Lennard River where it carved the magnificent limestone walls of Windjana Gorge into the Napier Range.

opposite: The wide sweep of Eighty Mile Beach gleams golden as the sun sets below the horizon. *above:* The symmetrical lines of Carlton Ridge, also known as the Sleeping Buddha, are reflected in the waters of Lake Kununurra.

opposite: The Bungle Bungles in Purnululu National Park. *above, left and right:* From the ground, the huge, rounded, banded domes stand out against the vivid blue dry-season skies, the rocks' shapes echoed in the smooth pebbles and in the rock ridges of the dry river bed.

pages 148 and 149: On the cliffs of Geikie Gorge, a line between the yellow of the lower cliff-face and the higher weathered brown rock marks the water level when wet season floods surge through this wide gorge.
above: The town of Marble Bar is named for this multi-coloured bar of jasper on the nearby Coongan River.

above: Mt Augustus, also known as Burringurrah, is twice the size of Central Australia's Uluru. Like Uluru, its colour changes with distance and time of day. When first sighted in the far distance it is a soft pale blue silhouette, and in the warm light of sunrise and sunset, the rock has an intensely red hue.

above: The huge rugged plateau of the Hamersley Range is home to Karijini National Park. The top of this plateau is mostly a gently undulating landscape, rounded hills of red rock, golden spinifex and white-barked Ghost Gums.

above: Unlike the subtle, gradual climb onto the plateau from the south, the northern edge of the Hamersley Range is a long wall of cliffs and deep gorges that finally break out onto the lowland plains. Karijini National Park is mostly on the plateau, with access to its spectacular gorges from above.

above: After rain, brightly coloured Sturt's Desert Pea spreads its lush green across ground that is bare, stony and almost as red as its flowers.

above: Karijini National Park is filled with waterfalls, wildlife and spectacularly colourful gorges.
Beautiful Hamersley Gorge (main picture) is in the western part of the park.

above: At Joffre Falls a creek drops in a series of many small falls down a long flight of narrow ledges.

above: At Fortescue Falls, in Dales Gorge, a stream flows down a long cascade to a large pool.

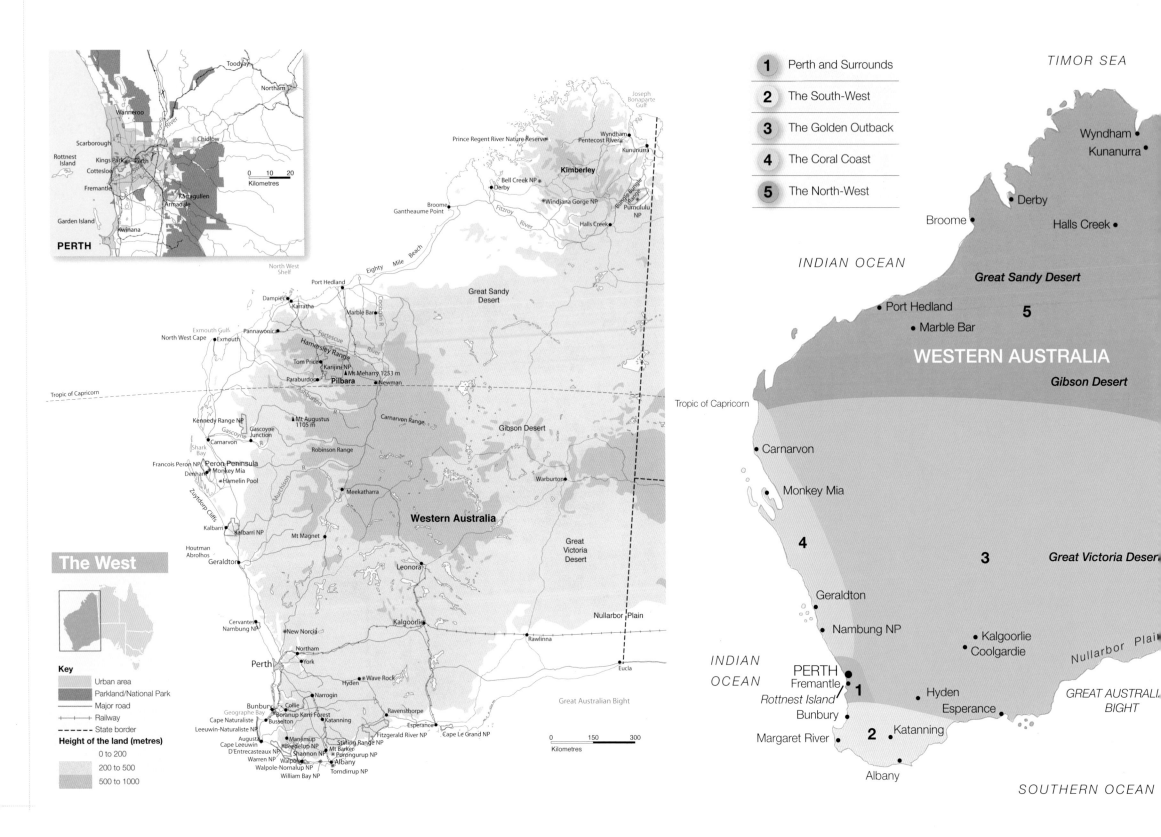

PERTH

Toodyay
Northam
Wanneroo
Scarborough
Chidlow
Rottnest
Island
Kings Park · Perth
Cottesloe
Fremantle
Karragullen
Armadale
Garden Island
Kwinana

0   10   20
Kilometres

The West

Key
- Urban area
- Parkland/National Park
- Major road
- Railway
- State border

Height of the land (metres)
- 0 to 200
- 200 to 500
- 500 to 1000

Joseph
Bonaparte
Gulf

Prince Regent River Nature Reserve

Wyndham
Pentecost River
Kununurra

Kimberley

Bell Creek NP
Derby
Windjana Gorge NP
Bungle Bungle Range
Purnululu
NP
Halls Creek

Broome
Gantheaume Point
Fitzroy River

North West
Shelf
Eighty Mile Beach

Port Hedland

**Great Sandy
Desert**

Dampier
Karratha
Marble Bar
Oakover R

Exmouth Gulf
Pannawonica
North West Cape
Exmouth
Fortescue River
Hamersley Range
Tom Price
Karijini NP
Mt Meharry 1253 m
Paraburdoo
Pilbara
Newman
Ashburton R

Tropic of Capricorn

Kennedy Range NP
Mt Augustus
1105 m
Carnarvon Range
Gascoyne
Junction
Gascoyne R
Carnarvon
Robinson Range
Gibson Desert
Shark
Bay
Francois Peron NP
Peron Peninsula
Murchison R
Monkey Mia
Denham
Hamelin Pool
Warburton

Meekatharra

Western Australia

Zuytdorp Cliffs

Kalbarri
Kalbarri NP
Mt Magnet

Houtman
Abrolhos
Geraldton
Leonora
**Great
Victoria
Desert**

Kalgoorlie

Nullarbor Plain
Rawlinna

Cervantes
Nambung NP
New Norcia
Northam
Perth
York
Hyden
Wave Rock
Eucla

Great Australian Bight

0   150   300
Kilometres

Bunbury
Collie
Narrogin
Geographe Bay
Boranup Karri Forest
Cape Naturaliste
Busselton
Katanning
Leeuwin-Naturaliste NP
Ravensthorpe
Fitzgerald River NP
Cape Le Grand NP
Esperance
Augusta
Manjimup
Stirling Range NP
Cape Leeuwin
Beedelup NP
Mt Barker
D'Entrecasteaux NP
Shannon NP
Porongurup NP
Warren NP
Walpole
Albany
Walpole-Nornalup NP
Torndirrup NP
William Bay NP

---

1 Perth and Surrounds
2 The South-West
3 The Golden Outback
4 The Coral Coast
5 The North-West

TIMOR SEA

Wyndham
Kunanurra

INDIAN OCEAN

Derby
Broome
Halls Creek

Great Sandy Desert

Port Hedland
Marble Bar

5

WESTERN AUSTRALIA

Gibson Desert

Tropic of Capricorn

Carnarvon

Monkey Mia

4

3

Great Victoria Desert

Geraldton

Nambung NP

Kalgoorlie
Coolgardie

Nullarbor Plain

INDIAN
OCEAN

PERTH
Fremantle
Rottnest Island
1

Hyden

Bunbury

Esperance

GREAT AUSTRALIAN
BIGHT

Margaret River

2 Katanning

Albany

SOUTHERN OCEAN

Index

above: Australian Sea-lions on a beach in the Houtman Abrolhos.

Published by Steve Parish Publishing Pty Ltd
PO Box 1058, Archerfield, Queensland 4108 Australia

© copyright Steve Parish Publishing Pty Ltd

ISBN 9781740215688

First published 2005. Reprinted 2007, 2010.

Photography: Steve Parish

Additional photography: p. 24 (right): AAP/Sport the Library; pp. 118–119: Ron & Valerie Taylor; p. 119 (right): Clay Bryce/Lochman Transparencies; p. 120 (left): G. Saueracker/Lochman Transparencies; p. 120 (right): Eva Boogaard/Lochman Transparencies; p. 121: G. Saueracker/Lochman Transparencies

Text: Michael Morcombe

Design: Leanne Staff and Gill Stack

Maps supplied by MAPgraphics, Australia

Prepress by Colour Chiefs Digital Imaging, Brisbane, Australia
Printed in China by Printplus Limited

Produced in Australia at the Steve Parish Publishing Studios

www.steveparish.com.au
www.photographaustralia.com.au